A Little Book About Skiing Better

"Feeling the Difference"

Jim Vigani
Joan Heaton

Barbara-Gayle Publishing, Inc.
Pittsburgh, PA

Barbara-Gayle Publishing, Inc.
101 Merrie Woode Drive
Pittsburgh, PA 15235-5142

ISBN: 978-0-9677026-3-6

For all the passionate and dedicated skiers who simply want to learn to ski better.

Thanks to:

- The Windham Mountain Snow Sports School and Franz Krickl, our director, for giving us the opportunity to test our theories and to develop our program.

- David A. Kolb, American Educational Theorist, for inspiring and for providing us with the foundation for our work.

- Marilyn H. Whalen, English Teacher - Grammarian and our editor, for all her endless review and editing.

- Kathleen W. Schmidt, our recreational skier, for giving us her practical and honest opinions of our work in her review of our book.

- Christine Vigani, Jim's wife, for her many critiques and unwavering support.

- Edward "Eddie" Kiziukiewicz, our friend, for his loyalty to our cause and for his steadfast support as we develop our program.

- Shawn Smith, Director of Resort Services, Stevens Pass, Skykomish, Washington; Former Coach and Member of the PSIA U.S. Alpine Demonstration Team, for reviewing our work and making helpful and insightful comments and suggestions.

- The Watchung Amateur Ski Club for starting Jim on his ski teaching career.

- The City College of New York for giving Joan the opportunity to start her ski teaching career.

Contents

Foreword –
How It All Started

There are times in life when **stuff** just happens – you know, that unplanned set of circumstances that changes the way you think. For years before we met, Joan and I had been working on improving our skiing and teaching skills, both, however, in a very different approach and style. Joan was the college professor skilled in teaching/learning styles, feedback, and class management. I was the engineer, analytical to the core, looking at the minutia of movements that good skiers made and trying to emulate them. We both had successes, but progress for both of us was painstakingly slow. We were both asking ourselves the same question, "Why was getting to ski better taking so long?"

When we finally got together at Windham in 1999, we immediately hit it off. Our passion for the sport was obvious to each other, as was our need to share our experiences. We started skiing together and bouncing ideas back and forth – trying to find a way to learn faster. Along the way, Joan discovered David Kolb's Experiential Learning Model. I had moved my focus to one of simplification – finding out what really mattered from a technical standpoint. When we put the two together, things started to happen; and we were sure we were on to something special. Over the next several years, our work evolved into a simple, straightforward approach for learning to ski better that has proven to be successful beyond our wildest expectations.

Together, we believe that the program we have come up with is so simple, one needs only to try it to believe it. By combining Kolb's Experiential Learning Model with a simple, skiing-mechanics model, and a simple, easy-to-use prescriptive tool, we discovered that learning explodes. One caveat though – learning slows way down if you try to over-complicate the process by over-analyzing what you are doing, how you are moving, or by not following the Experiential Learning Model steps in order. We have had so much fun and success using this approach, we just had to share it with as many skiers as possible. This little book is our way of doing just that.

Some background information about Joan and Jim:

Joan Heaton has been teaching skiing professionally for some 30 years and is responsible for introducing the Teaching Styles into the Professional Ski Instructors of America (PSIA) curriculum. She is also the author of *A National Survey on Teacher Behavior in Ski Teaching*, PSIA, 1983; and *The Teaching Dimension*, PSIA-Eastern Division. She is a PSIA Certified Level II Instructor. At the time of this writing, Joan is working in the Windham Mountain Snow Sports School in New York as an Educational Consultant and Teacher Trainer. Joan is a retired Physical Education professor from The City College of the City University of New York with a broad background in teaching methodology.

Jim Vigani is a PSIA Certified Level III Instructor and a retired Divisional Clinic Leader (DCL) for PSIA-E. He has been teaching skiing professionally since 1975. Jim has been a ski school director, a technical director, and, currently, a training supervisor at Windham

Mountain Snow Sports School. He was also very active in the American Society for Testing and Materials (ASTM) for skiing safety standards development. Jim is a Forensic Engineer and President of his own technical consulting firm. A mechanical engineer by education, he has a very eclectic background.

As you read on, you may notice that some of the chapters are written in Joanie's voice, some in Jim's voice, and some in both. We felt using this heartfelt style helped us convey the passion we both have for what we want to share. You will also notice that many of the concepts are discussed a number of times throughout the book. We have done this so you don't have to necessarily read the chapters in order.

You should understand that this book is not intended to be the 'be all and do all' of learning to ski or for the never-ever skier. Rather, it is designed to set a foundation for recreational skiers to help them ski at advanced levels. It will also be useful to ski instructors as it provides a road map for understanding a student's problems and directing solutions. We hope you enjoy the read.

1

Throw Away Your Checklist

When I decided to join the Windham Mountain Snow Sports School, a ski-instructor friend named Peter said to me, "If you really want to improve your skiing, try to hook up with a guy named Jim Vigani." As a new member of the school, I set out to do just that. When the big day came, Jim and I took a run together and met at the bottom of the trail. I immediately apologized because I felt I hadn't skied my best since the trail just wasn't long enough for me to finish my **checklist**. I told Jim that I had a list of all the things I needed to do and that the trail we skied was just too short for me to get through my list. I simply needed more trail to make sure my hands, hips, shoulders, and other body parts were all in the right place – just where my list said they needed to be. Unfortunately, I am sure too many of you know exactly what I'm talking about. My list was written on yellow, legal-size paper with something on each line; and I carried it with me every time I skied. Did you know that there are 30 lines on a legal-size piece of paper?? When I told Jim about my list, he laughed. I tried to explain that what I really needed was to find a trail long enough for me to get through my checklist. Then, near the **end** of the run, he could see me at my best. I am not sure how to put Jim's reaction into words, or mine for that matter; but, HE TORE UP MY PRECIOUS LIST! All I know is that my prized checklist, the one that I had carefully prepared over the years, was now gone forever!

Before Jim tore up my list, my typical ski run would go something like this: hands forward, pelvis moving into the turn, outside shoulder and hand lower than the inside shoulder and hand, hold back my left hip, focus down the hill, stop tipping my shoulders in on my right turn, and on and on. As I skied, I would be concentrating so hard on trying to get my body into **the position** that any chance of actually getting my stance right, at the right time, was just a random happening. I was convinced that if I could just put my body parts where they needed to be, everything would be perfect.

After Jim tore up my list, we hopped on the chair to take another run. I was really nervous. I never skied without my list! On the way up, Jim told me a story about a **smart** student who changed the way Jim taught. The fellow was an intermediate skier named George. He took a lesson from Jim one day; and after watching George make a few turns, Jim said, "George, you are in the 'backseat'. You need to move your hips forward." George, taking it all in, asked, "How far forward?" "Wow," Jim thought, "this guy is smart." But then Jim thought to himself, "I'm smart, too," and Jim replied, "Just enough, George, just enough." In all his wisdom, George asked, "How do I know when it's just enough, Jim?" "Whew," thought Jim, "this guy is good!" But, not to be outdone, Jim replied, "When you can **feel** the tips of your skis engage the snow throughout the whole turn – that's when." It was at that moment Jim realized rather than having George worry about where his hips were, he could have simply taught George to **feel** the tips of his skis engage the snow and the whole conversation could have been avoided!

After the story, we both had a laugh; and Jim continued, "Joanie, you just can't worry about positioning your body parts or about trying to make pre-programmed movements. You need to learn to **feel** and to allow your body to move **just enough**. The concept is simple – Don't **make** a move, **let** the movement **happen**. **Let** your movements **evolve** situationally. **Feel** your skis in the moment and allow your body to respond to that moment. As you ski, it is literally impossible to pre-program your every movement. Things are constantly changing and a movement that might have been appropriate three feet back isn't appropriate **NOW**."

What Jim said made so much sense! It was then that I was reminded of my graduate work in Motor Learning and what I learned about **Open and Closed Skills**. What Jim was describing was how we perform an **open** skill; and clearly, skiing is an open skill. I had been approaching skiing as a **closed** skill. A good example of a closed skill is shooting a foul shot in basketball. In the NBA, the basket is always

18 inches in diameter and 10 feet above the floor. The backboard is 15 feet from the foul line and no one can bother the shooter. Closed Skills are best mastered by practicing in repetitions (a lot!) and working toward gaining so called 'muscle memory.' Watch an NBA player when he steps up to the foul line. He does exactly the same thing every time he shoots a foul shot – he stands exactly in the same spot, twirls the ball twice, bounces it five times, and finally, takes the shot. Players like this stand at the foul line for hours practicing the same programmed movements that will get them a successful foul shot. They can do this because the situation never changes.

In contrast, an open skill takes place when conditions are constantly changing. It requires that decisions and adjustments be made **on the run**. A good example of an open skill is a quarterback throwing a forward pass. Based on the location of the downfield defensive players, the quarterback must constantly make adjustments, determine who he's going to throw to, all the while trying to avoid being tackled. You only have to go skiing once to understand that skiing is an open skill. As we move down the hill, conditions are constantly changing: the texture of the snow, the slope of the hill, the other skiers around us... It all keeps changing. And, on top of all this, as things are changing, their importance to the skier, at any particular moment, changes as well. Now, that's a lot to handle. So, how do we begin to manage all that's happening around us as we ski? If you attempt to come up with pre-programmed movements or try to think of where all your different body parts should be for a particular situation, as I was trying to do, you will surely find that by the time you make the movement, you're too late!

Well, Jim was thrilled with this information. And, I was happy, too! Jim began to understand why what he was doing worked, and I understood where he was coming from. We both saw the connection between the openness of the skills of skiing and how the explanation of Open and Closed Skills made everything make sense. It explains how trying to pre-program movements in skiing limits your success: you just can't predict what the mountain will throw at you as you move down the hill. Jim is famous for the hand demonstration he does as he describes skiing and the mountain – when the mountain demands **this** (and he vertically opens and closes the thumb and forefinger of his right hand), you are fine if you do **this** (he repeats the same demonstration with his left hand.) However, when the mountain changes and requires you to do **this** (he tilts his right hand horizontally and opens and closes his fingers), you can't keep doing **this** (he keeps the fingers of his left hand moving vertically). If you do, you'll be in trouble. You just can't keep doing the same thing when the situation changes. You need to change as the situation demands. Believe me, that's **Open Skill** country! So, **THROW AWAY YOUR CHECKLIST** and get in the **NOW!**

2

It's All About Balance!

If you have been skiing for any length of time, the word 'BALANCE' surely has come up as a topic of discussion with peers or in any lesson you may have taken. Everybody talks about it. They say it's the 'mother' of all skiing skills and an absolute necessity for good skiing. Many skiers run through a myriad of drills and exercises aimed at improving their balance. And yet, when we watch people ski, almost all of them are **out-of-balance.** Why? The answer is simple. Very few people actually know what it **feels** like to be **in-balance** while they're skiing. To become a good skier, it is imperative that we understand and know what it feels like to be in **dynamic** balance!

That being said, what's this balance stuff really all about? The first thing we need to understand is the difference between **static** and **dynamic** balance. If you are standing in the lift line waiting to get on the lift and you don't fall over, you are in static balance. The only major force you're dealing with is gravity. However, once you get off the lift and start moving down the hill, everything changes. This is when **dynamic balancing** kicks in. Not only are you dealing with gravity, you are also dealing with the dynamics of motion including: friction, momentum, lateral acceleration, centripetal force, etc. That's a lot to deal with and way too much to think about. Managing and using these dynamics of motion **without thinking** is the mark of a good skier.

Just because you don't fall over when you're moving, doesn't mean you are in **dynamic** balance. It just means you didn't fall over. So, you might ask, "How do you know when you are in **dynamic** balance?" The answer is surprisingly simple – you are in **dynamic** balance when you can make your skis do what you want them to do, when you want them to do it! It's being in that **state** where you can move when, where, and how you need to move. Every one of us has had the experience, especially in the moguls, when we wanted to turn **here,** but we couldn't. We were stuck! The reason we were stuck was that we were **out-of-balance**. The task then becomes learning to feel and recognize when you are **in-balance** and when you are getting **out-of-balance**. Learning to keep yourself in that **state** where you don't get **stuck** is the name of the game.

One very important point – learn to balance from your core, not on your feet. Your core is that spot somewhere near and behind your navel that is often called your center of gravity. One of the best examples of balancing from the core can be seen when watching a good track star running the hurdles. As he moves from running on the track to vaulting over the hurdles, his balance continues to be centered at his core. It doesn't matter if his feet are touching the ground or not, he remains **in-balance.** And so it is with skiing. Balancing from the core gives you a freedom to move when and how you want.

BALANCE vs. BALANCING –
What's the difference?

Everyone is born with their own unique sense of balance – that ability to recognize when they are **in or out-of-balance**. Those with a keen sense of balance can feel very small variations in their state of balance. Others are not so lucky. For those people, it takes more of an effort to recognize the **difference** between being **in and out-of-balance**.

While being **in-balance** is the **state** we strive for, **balance-'ing'** is the action we take to maintain that balance. These actions are the balancing skills. The bad news is that we have to live with whatever sense of balance we were born with. The good news is that we can train, develop, and improve our balancing skills.

Very rarely are we in perfect balance as we ski. However, the closer we get to that state of perfect balance, the better everything gets. By developing our balancing skills, we can vastly improve our ability to recognize, within the limits of our own unique sense of balance, what needs to be done to stay closer to that perfect state. Many of the tasks outlined in **Chapter 10, Tasks Every 'Good' Skier Can Do**, are designed just for that purpose.

There are three fundamental balancing skills that need to be developed in order to improve our skiing: Fore-Aft (front to back), Lateral (side to side), and Vertical (up and down). We have found that by working primarily on fore-aft and lateral balancing, vertical balancing, generally, falls into place.

While maintaining a near perfect state of balance is a lofty goal, most of us just can't devote enough time on the snow to ever actually get there. However, as we learn to balance **better**, there are training tactics we can use that can bring us close.

In our approach, we generally train fore-aft balance first. While conventional wisdom says optimum fore-aft balance emanates from a middle-of-the-foot stance, we begin, tactically, by first teaching balancing further forward off the ball of the foot. This forward-biased, **home** stance provides a multitude of benefits to the learner. The primary benefit is that, generally, it is a safer way to ski. Skiing out-of-balance to the rear often creates serious control problems with unwanted acceleration. If you lack the skills to consistently ski from the middle-of-the-foot and you get knocked back, you will be out-of-balance to the rear, with the inevitable lack of control. If you tactically balance with a forward-bias and get knocked back, more often than not, you will only go back to the middle. This is not such a bad place to be as you will still have a stance that allows you to stay in control. A bit of advice here – before you attempt any change of direction, you need to **find home!** Racing coaches call this **re-centering.** As your fore-aft balancing skills improve, you can move your **home** stance more to the middle of your foot to squeeze the most performance out of your skis. However, even if you never get to that mid-foot **home** stance, you can still do very well by using the tactic of a forward-biased stance.

We approach improving lateral balancing with a similar tactic. Once again, conventional wisdom would say – balance laterally using both feet. However, we begin, tactically, by teaching balancing on the outside foot/ski (commonly referred to as standing on the downhill ski) of the turn. This outside-ski-bias provides a solid platform on which to move, making it easier to resist leaning into the hill. Leaning into the hill causes your skis to slip out from under you, particularly on steep hills and harder snow. Once you have mastered balancing on the outside foot, you can then move on to a more two-footed stance with both skis working efficiently. However, you can still get to be a pretty good skier by using the tactic of balancing predominately on the outside foot/ski.

Generally, vertical balancing skills become more essential as the terrain gets more difficult and/or your speed increases. We have found that by the time your fore-aft and lateral balancing skills have developed to the point where speed and terrain are not an issue, your vertical balancing skills will have followed along nicely. Generally, only at the highest levels of skiing, which are not the primary focus of this book, do we consider specifically training vertical balancing skills.

Focusing on improving your balancing skills should be at the heart of your program to improve your skiing. It truly is **ALL ABOUT BALANCE!**

3

Simplifying the Mechanics of Skiing

It's amazing how much insight you can get just by asking questions. One afternoon, after skiing, we were all at the bar when we got into a technical discussion regarding the phases of a ski turn. At the time, most everyone agreed there were three phases of a turn: the initiation phase, the controlling phase, and the completion phase.

The discussion was starting to get a little technical; however, it seemed interesting enough, so we hung in there. The discussion continued as we tried to describe and understand all the things that go on during these three phases and where those things occurred. This is when it started to get a bit much. The common thinking was that the initiation phase began at the transition between turns and continued just before you entered the fall line. During this phase, you needed to stand up (extend) and flatten your skis on the snow while moving forward, diagonally into the new turn. As you changed from one set of corresponding edges to the other, you entered the controlling phase during which you passed through the fall line, reaching your maximum extension and establishing appropriate angulation. As you continued turning, you entered the completion phase of the turn where the pressure on your skis reached its maximum, requiring appropriate flexing to manage that pressure, all the time setting up for the initiation phase of the next turn. Good skiing was nothing more than linking a series of these three phases, all the time scribing a series of "C" shaped turns in the snow as you moved down the hill.

Simple enough? RIGHT! Well, not for me. I asked a simple question, "Just suppose I started a new turn with a perfect execution of the initiation phase. As I continued into and through the controlling phase, perfectly executing every required movement, another skier cut me off and I had to instantly change direction. What happened to my completion phase? Where did it go?" We laughed as we thought about it and the answer became clear. If you are in-balance, at any point in your turn, you should be able to start changing direction if you wanted. Or, you could just continue turning. That being the case, when you are in-balance, at any point along your turn you are potentially in any one of the three phases. The phase that you were actually in would depend upon what you did next. So what we discovered was that although it was interesting and fun to get into the minutia of the mechanics, this very technical approach became overwhelming and performance limiting when actually skiing. All agreed there had to be a simpler way. Enter **The Simplified Mechanics of Skiing**.

The idea of **The Simplified Mechanics of Skiing** evolved from my frustration of knowing that, while I had a high level of understanding of the technical aspects of skiing, my skiing was improving at a painstakingly slow pace. There just had to be another way. Here is when asking another question changed my skiing. The question I asked myself was, "If I had to consider the three most important areas to focus on to improve my skiing, what would they be?" Learning to balance, of course, was the first thing that came to mind. It was very clear that if I were in-balance, I could do just about anything I wanted with my skis, any time I wanted. Being in-balance then, was an absolute necessity if I were to have the ability and options to adjust for all those variable situations I would encounter on my way down the hill.

My first principle then became – **If you're not in-balance, nothing else matters. Understanding** what **being in-balance** meant was another question I asked myself. I surely had to know how to recognize when I was in-balance and when I was not. To make a long story short, I discovered that when I was in-balance, I could start a change of direction any time I wanted. If I couldn't, I knew I was out-of-balance. I'm sure we have all had the experience, especially in the moguls, when we wanted to turn NOW, but we couldn't. We were stuck! We were out-of-balance. Being in-balance, then, is putting and keeping yourself in that state where you don't get stuck. It's a **feeling** rather than a **position**. Let your body move however it needs to move to get and maintain that feeling.

Let's get a little technical here for a second. We need to understand that the overall skill of balancing has three sub-skills: Fore-Aft, Lateral, and Vertical. As I continued asking questions, I realized that each of these sub-skills had its own importance.

Focusing on lateral balance, I realized that while the importance of the inside ski, particularly with the newer shaped skis, is a matter of great discussion among skiers, there seems to be a lot of misunderstanding relating to the topic. As a result, many skiers attempt to ski 'on' both feet, rather than 'with' both feet. However, my experience tells me that the outside ski of a turn is the controlling ski, while the inside ski complements and augments the dynamics of the turn. Consequently, the ability to balance on the outside ski gives me the option to control exactly what the inside ski is doing, optimizing its effect throughout the turn. Skiing 'with' both feet, in proper lateral balance, allows each ski to be used independently throughout the turn. Skiing 'on' both feet limits that independence. It is like trying to walk while keeping both feet always on the ground.

My second principle then became – **Learn to balance on the outside ski first.** Only after you learn to balance on the outside ski can the inside ski be used effectively. As an aside, even if you just learn to balance predominately on the outside ski, you can still get to be a pretty good skier.

When I thought about the times I got into trouble, the most common mistake I made was sitting-back. This is commonly called **being in the 'backseat'.** I noticed I wasn't alone! Skiing in the backseat is perhaps the single most deleterious cause of mediocre skiing. It is the curse of the less accomplished skier and is the foremost symptom of being out of fore-aft balance. My next question then was, "What can I do to maintain my fore-aft balance without worrying about how I **should** be moving?" Advice like 'keep your hips over your feet', 'dive into the turn', 'keep your hands forward' didn't seem to really help much. By watching the best skiers and by studying lots of videos and photographs, it became clear to me that most turns started with the engagement of the ski tips in the snow. How these skiers moved depended on the situation – the type of turn, the terrain, the speed, the snow condition, etc. There was no single movement pattern that was used all the time. What was clear, though, was that **how** they moved resulted in the tips of the skis engaging in the snow. They were definitely not in the backseat. My third principle then became – **Move to engage the tips.** Since you can't engage the tips of your skis from the backseat, learning to 'move to engage the tips' was what I needed to do. I also recognized that, while good skiers **started** a turn by engaging the tips of their skis, they could also **keep** the tips engaged throughout the entire turn. It's not that they skied with their tips engaged all the time, but it's that they **could** if they chose. So, if you want to give your skiing a boost, learn how to start a turn by 'moving to engage the tips and keeping them engaged throughout the entire turn.' Having this skill allows you to **work** the ski along its length while being able to get to the front of the skis when you need to. It is the best cure I have found for the 'backseat blues.'

Anyone who has skied at all knows there are many other things that are going on as you ski. However, I found that those **other things** are mostly details. Details that only become important after you have built a strong foundation based on the first three principles of the Simplified Mechanics. My final principle then became – **Everything else is a detail.** For example, I see many out-of-balance skiers trying to keep their hands forward, as if simply holding the hands forward was the holy grail of skiing. They often compensate by pushing their butt further back keeping them out-of-balance. Nothing really changed. Another detail is learning how to use your poles. Knowing how and where to plant your pole, while very important to the more accomplished skier, has little benefit if you are out-of-balance and unable to turn when and where you want. Skiers in-balance can make some pretty nice turns without ever planting their poles. Build your foundation first and then add the details.

So here it is in a nutshell:

The Simplified Mechanics of Skiing

- _If you're not in-balance, nothing else matters._
- _Learn to balance on the outside ski first._
- _Move to engage the tips._
- _Everything else is a detail._

4

Know Your Starting Point

Some time ago I was working with my coach trying to make a certain type of turn. At first, I just couldn't do it. Finally, on one attempt, somehow, I did it. "That's it," he yelled. "That's it. Did you **feel** the difference that time?" "What difference?" I said, "Seemed the same to me." And, under my breath, I said to myself, "I'm trying to do something here: what's this **feeling** stuff all about? Why didn't he just tell me what I did so I could do it again? How was I supposed to know what I did if he didn't tell me?" That's when the proverbial light bulb went on. I finally realized that for all too long I had been focusing on trying to make perfect movements and trying to position my body parts the way I saw the very best skiers in photographs and in videos doing it. What I really **needed** to do was focus on **feeling** what my skis were doing. I had to learn to feel what they were doing to begin with, so I could feel **when** and **if** I got them to do something else. I finally figured a way to recognize the difference. **I HAD TO BECOME A FEELER FIRST!**

Here's another story from my viewpoint as an instructor. This past season I found my way to teaching in the Adult Program in our snow sports school. Five ladies were assigned to my class; each had a passion for skiing and a desire to learn to ski better. On the first day, I asked them which trails they enjoyed skiing as I needed to have an idea of what to expect from them skill-wise. We took that first run and, while all seemed to be going smoothly, I could see their fear of the fall line as all five ladies rushed to make that dreaded ole 'Z' turn. As we continued to ski, I asked one of the ladies what she was trying to do. She answered, "Slow down." I then asked, "How are you trying to do that?" She said, "Well, I know I need to keep my hands forward, face my body down the hill, and dig in my edges." I said to myself, "Been there, done that!" Then I asked her, "What does it **feel** like when you do that?" She responded,

"I don't know, I never thought about it like that." My goal became clear: I had to get my ladies to **feel** what they and their skis were doing – their **starting point**. Without a starting point, it would be difficult to move them to another point.

When you ask skiers if they feel what's happening when they ski, the usual answers are something like, "Yes, No, and What do you mean?" Certainly, while they are probably **feeling** something, most are not really **feelers** in the context of what's needed when we ski.

To become the **feeler** we are talking about, you need to develop an awareness of what is happening **NOW**. That is, being able to sense what is happening in the moment, both with your body and with your skis, and **associating** those sensations with an **outcome**.

The good news is that we **can** teach ourselves to become feelers, and, at first, it really doesn't matter if the outcome is good, bad, or otherwise. What does matter is that you have made the association between a sensation and an outcome. This done, you have established a place to begin – your **starting point**.

On a personal note, I have to say that I was so proud of myself when I experienced my first, real **NOW** moment. I was trying to carve throughout an entire turn and, for once, I was not focusing on making perfect movements; but instead, I was focusing on what I felt my skis were doing. At times, believe it or not, I could feel my skis 'hooking-up' and starting to carve. For the first time, I could actually feel the difference between a 'carving' ski and a 'skidding' ski. I was finally sensing what was happening to me in the **NOW** – that moment when I connected what I was feeling with what was actually happening. The more I focused on the sensations of carving, the easier carving became. This connection is called a **Concrete Experience** (see **Chapter 5, Supercharge Your Learning**).

A little background in learning theory here would be helpful. People typically learn physical activities in different ways. We call these ways, **styles of learning**. There are four basic styles of learning that people use: the kinesthetic learners (natural feelers), the analytical learners (thinkers), the observers (watchers), and the trial and error types (doers).

Most people tend to favor one of the learning styles (this is called their dominant style) at the expense of the other styles. However, if you want to move off that plateau that you've been on, at some point you need to learn through the **feeling style**. It becomes 'a learn to learn' thing! As a caveat, you will see in **Chapter 5, Supercharge Your Learning**, that you can actually teach yourself to learn in all four learning styles and, as a result, **supercharge your learning**.

In our many years as ski instructors, helping someone to truly become a **feeler** has been one of our greatest challenges. Ask me how I know this? **I** thought **I** would be on a plateau **forever**! Then I 'learned to learn' to be a feeler. I encourage you to take the leap as I did and expand beyond your dominant learning style and 'learn to learn' in all four styles. It can be a scary experience, but it's worth it! We have found there are those who resist, those who pretend, and those who make the leap. Make the leap! **Learn to be a feeler first!**

5

Supercharge Your Learning
– The Kolb Model –

Mark had the reputation of being one of the best ski instructors in the country. When he worked with me, he knew that I read a lot about skiing and that I was very analytical. He knew that I was a **Thinker**. I knew he was familiar with the different styles of learning (Feeler, Watcher, Thinker, Doer), and I liked how he worked with me knowing that I was a thinker. Everything he did catered to my dominant learning style, and I took in his every word like a sponge. As much as I liked the way he taught, my problem was that learning to ski better was taking me way too long. Well, that was until I discovered the work of David A. Kolb!

I know, you're asking, "Who is David Kolb?" Since my story is not such a long one, I think it's worth telling. A number of years ago, the technical director of our snow sports school asked me to do a presentation for our school on Experiential Teaching. That was the **buzz** phrase that year. As I researched the project, I couldn't find a whole lot on Experiential Teaching; but I did find a lot on Teaching for Experiential Learning, a learning model developed by David Kolb.

David A. Kolb is a professor in the Department of Organizational Behavior in the Weatherhead School of Management at Case Western Reserve University in Cleveland, Ohio. In 1971, in an effort to improve the learning process, Professor Kolb started to work on his Experiential Learning Theory (ELT). The model he developed is a holistic approach to learning based on experience and practical application. I was very excited when I saw his model because it seemed like the perfect approach for accelerating the learning process. I showed the model to Jim and he immediately saw how powerful it was. Based on what we knew, we started shaping a ski teaching methodology around the model.

Our work started with Kolb's description of his four stage learning model consisting of:
- Stage 1 – Concrete Experience
- Stage 2 – Observation and Reflection
- Stage 3 – Formation of Abstract Concepts, and Generalizations
- Stage 4 – Testing Implication of Concepts in New Situations.

What was exciting for us was how the four stages lined up with the four learning styles we talked about in **Chapter 4, Know Your Starting Point**. We were also excited to discover how going through the model actually expanded a person's learning because they were using all four learning styles, not just one.

- Concrete Experience – learning through 'Feeling.'
- Observation and Reflection – learning by 'Watching.'

- Formation of Abstract Concepts, and Generalizations – learning through 'Thinking.'
- Testing Implication of Concepts in New Situations – learning by 'Doing.'

Professor Kolb determined that learning is accelerated when a student goes through all four stages in their stated order. If you remember in **Chapter 4, Know Your Starting Point**, we discussed the need to have a starting point. Kolb's model fit right into our thinking by providing that starting point. However, it went much further because it outlined a complete learning cycle that we found easy to follow.

In our adoption of Kolb's model to skiing, Experiential Learning **must** start with the **Concrete Experience** (Stage 1). This concrete experience is an awareness of the **NOW.** It is sensing what is happening in the moment with your body and your skis as you perform a task and connecting those sensations with what **actually** happens. This connection of sensations with what is actually happening is what creates the concrete experience. Without that connection, there is no physical reference for the experience and no starting point for change.

In Stage 2, we decide if what actually happened was what we wanted to happen. If it was, all is good – we know what that particular outcome feels like and we have a good chance of repeating it when we want to. If not, we move on to Stage 3. In Stage 3, we try to figure out what we might change to get the result we really wanted. This generally involves altering the task. With our newly altered task in hand, we enter Stage 4 where we try again. As we perform the new task, we experience new sensations, connect these sensations with the new results, and create a new concrete experience. And the cycle begins again! One note of advice here – in Stages 2 and 3, a good coach can be helpful. In Stage 2, the coach helps you figure out what actually happened as compared to what you wanted to happen. In Stage 3, the coach will help to figure out how the task might be altered to try to get the desired result. As you will see in **Chapter 6, What Am I Doing Wrong?**, your coach should not try to tell you **how** to perform the task. Your coach's job is to guide you through the experience, while letting **you** figure out what needs to be done.

Once you get the hang of it, going through Kolb's model is actually a simple and natural process. The diagram that follows shows how a learner cycles though the model in an ever-continuing upward learning spiral.

Cycling Through the Stages
of Kolb's Model

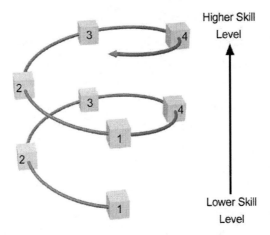

Key:
1. Concrete Experience
2. Observation and Reflection
3. Formation of Abstract Concepts and Generalizations
4. Testing Implications of Concepts in New Situations

Some learners instinctively do this – they feel, they reflect, they analyze, and they try again. If you are one of these learners, great; if not, give the model a try.

Let's just walk through the model as you try to learn to carve your skis. You decide that you should start in a shallow traverse. As you push off and move across the hill, you need to pay close attention to what you are feeling. Now, if you connect those feelings with what your skis are doing, you have completed Stage 1. You have had your **Concrete Experience!** Believe it or not, at this point, it doesn't really matter whether your skis were carving or not. The important part is that you connected your feelings with **whatever** your skis were doing.

Moving on to Stage 2, you need to determine whether or not your skis were actually carving (observing). This is where a good coach can help. If your skis were carving, everything is copasetic and you now know what a carving ski feels like. If they weren't, something needs to change. On to Stage 3...

In Stage 3, you (and your coach) figure out your strategy for change (thinking). The best way to do this is to 'alter or modify the task;' that is, try the task in a slightly different fashion. For example, you may have initially tried the traverse while standing on both skis. The modified task might involve trying the traverse again, but this time, standing with 100% of your weight on your downhill ski.

In Stage 4, you try or test your modified task (doing). During this testing, you will have new sensations and a new result. By connecting the new sensations with the new result, you have a new concrete experience; and the cycle begins again. It's important that you don't get trapped into trying to put your body parts into a **correct** position. Rather, you need to focus on your feelings and associate them with the results. Just allow your body to move however it needs to move. Repeating the process will quickly bring you to a place where you can repeat the feelings/sensations necessary to make your skis carve.

After we discovered and worked with Kolb's model, we couldn't believe how much learning was accelerated. As we mentioned above, a coach can help, not by **telling** you what to do, but rather, by **helping** you in Stages 2 and 3. It always helps to have a trained set of eyes to figure out what is happening (Stage 2) and to help you come up with alternate tasks (Stage 3).

So, there you have it. While Kolb's model may seem a bit technical, the process is straightforward and actually very logical. It is, without doubt, the most powerful learning tool we have ever used. Give it a try and **SUPERCHARGE YOUR LEARNING!**

6

What Am I Doing Wrong?

"What am I doing wrong?" is the most common question ski instructors hear. And, like so many other things in our approach, our answer to that question is simply, "It depends." Not exactly what the person asking the question wants to hear. The more useful question is, "Is what is happening what I want to happen?" The answer is, "If what you want to happen is happening, then you **are** doing it **right**. If not, you're doing it **wrong**." What we like about our approach is the freedom it brings to your skiing. Just think about it – how often has some critic told you how you **should** look when you ski; what you **should** be doing with your hands, hips, shoulders, etc.; or how your skis **should** go over the snow? If you've been skiing for any length of time, we're sure very often. While the quest to make those **perfect ski - book** turns, turn after turn down the mountain, may be a lofty goal, this approach tends to make skiing much more serious than it needs to be; and, surely, it takes away a lot of the spontaneity.

If you really take notice, you will discover that a lot of good skiers do make nice, controlled, round turns time after time. You watch them ski down the hill and you say to yourself, "Yeah, that guy is good." However, a **great** skier, in our opinion, dances down the hill playing with the snow and terrain in a spontaneous choreography of movement controlled only by the skier's imagination and the willingness of the mountain to cooperate. In that milieu, function and style come together in a unique way not possible with the **trying to make perfect turns** attitude and the **what am I doing wrong** approach. Keep in mind that while there are basic fundamentals that you need to understand and learn, you can and should create your own individual style, whatever that might be.

Here's a story to make this point. One year at training, I was skiing with a partner. I was leading and he was following. His task was to watch me and critique my skiing. About half way down the slope, I stopped to hear his comments. The first thing he said, with a look and tone of concern, was, "Your skis are coming off the snow!" I responded, "I know. Watch me again." When we got to the bottom, I turned to him and said, "Now they're not." It was very clear that my partner was more concerned with how my style fit into his 'always make perfect turns' approach, rather than trying to appreciate or understand what **I** was doing and how **I** might be doing it. Before telling me what he thought I was doing **wrong**, he should have asked me, "What were you trying to do?" Instead, he pre-judged my skiing according to his idea of how a skier should look. We have been told that to ski efficiently, we need to keep our skis on the snow. While this may be true, at that particular moment, I wasn't all that concerned about being efficient. Personally, I enjoy when my skis rebound off the snow. I like the **feel** of the ski releasing its energy and the reaction of my body to that release. In the above example, I was making my skis come off the snow **on purpose**. What was happening was what I wanted to happen. So, what I **was** doing was **right**!

Having what we want to happen actually happen, then, becomes our primary goal. (See **Chapter 10, Tasks Every 'Good' Skier Can Do** for guidance here.) This is where understanding what we discussed in **Chapter 4, Know Your Starting Point**, becomes important. Learning to **feel** what your skis are doing is the key to figuring out what is happening.

The 'traditional' approach of error detection and correction, otherwise known as the **What am I doing wrong?** approach, more often than not, focuses on symptoms rather than the cause of a problem. This approach is the seed of the checklist syndrome we discussed in **Chapter 1, Throw Away Your Checklist**. Since we threw away our checklist, we need to figure a way to address the actual **cause** of a problem, not just a symptom.

Our first step then is to understand that a problem only exists if what is happening isn't what you want to happen. The question then becomes, "What is the root cause of **it** not happening?" Our experience has shown that **almost all problems skiers have can be traced to one or a combination of only three issues: fore-aft balance, lateral balance, or tactics**. Identifying which issue(s) causes the problem gives you a clear and simple path to follow: the path being, focusing on improving your balancing and tactical skill(s) deficiencies that cause the problem. This approach then becomes our **Prescription Model.** Understanding this model greatly simplifies your ability to focus on those areas and skills that give you the most 'bang for your buck.' Working on these three areas alone will improve your skiing an order of magnitude.

For example, it should be obvious that chronic sitting-back is a clear fore-aft balance issue. However, if you are sitting-back, trying to follow the 'traditional' advice such as 'just move your hips forward more over your feet' is really just focusing on a symptom of your sitting-back. It doesn't address the root cause, which is your inability to balance while moving forward. If you just try to move your hips forward, the question becomes, "How far forward?" The answer, of course, is, "It depends!" (You've heard that before.) When properly balanced fore-aft, your hips will be exactly where they need to be at any moment in time. Learning to recognize when you are getting out of fore-aft balance and then to quickly get back into fore-aft balance eliminates sitting-back. It's as simple as that.

Other examples of symptoms versus causes are:

- Rotating the upper body to start a turn is generally seen as a root cause; when, in fact, it is most often the symptom of a deeper problem – that being a fore-aft balance issue. If a skier does not move forward when he/she wants to start a turn, the tips of the skis never engage the snow, and the skis don't want to change direction. The skier then has to resort to some kind of gross body movement to get the skis to go around the corner. Most typically, it's upper body rotation, a very powerful twisting force. In fact, it's so powerful that, once started, it's hard to stop. The skier generally ends up finishing the turn facing up the hill, out-of-balance, and ill-prepared to start another turn.

- Assuming the skier's skis are sharp, uncontrolled slipping sideways is also a symptom. It's typically combined with tipping or leaning 'into the hill.' In most cases, the root cause is a lateral balance issue. Effective lateral balancing allows skiers to properly edge their skis to get the grip needed to prevent slipping.

Let's see how all this fits together. If you remember in **Chapter 2, It's All About Balance!**, we discussed the importance of understanding dynamic balance and improving your balancing skills. We also discussed how knowing how to dynamically balance on your skis gives you the options to make your skis do what you want, when you want, the way you want. The better balanced you are, the more options you have. Choosing the most appropriate of your available options in a specific situation becomes your tactical approach to the task at hand. Learning to balance provides the options, and experience provides the knowledge of tactics. So, it's not about **WHAT AM I DOING WRONG?**: it's about learning and doing what **YOU** want to do!

7

The Learning Triad
- A Plan of Action -

If you look at **Chapters 3, 5, and 6**, you'll see
that we have introduced a **Mechanics Model**, a
Learning Model, and a **Prescription Model**.
These three models comprise what we have
identified as **The Learning Triad**. This Triad
provides a basic framework that allows you to
accelerate your development as a skier as never
before. Learning to use the Triad gives you a
simple and direct road map for identifying
problems with your skiing and recognizing the
root causes of those problems while providing a
focus and plan of action to alleviate them. At

the same time, it develops the open skill set that skiing requires. We have to say that, based on our experience, **The Learning Triad's** simplicity is surpassed only by its effectiveness.

The 'traditional' approach to improving your skiing typically involves attempting to train your body to establish specific, pre-programmed movements, often called building 'muscle memory.' With this approach, your attention is typically focused on trying to match a practiced movement with the situation at hand. We have found that this **closed** focus on the movements and positioning of body parts actually interferes with the freedom needed to respond to the **openness** of the skiing venue. As we discussed in **Chapter 1, Throw Away Your Checklist**, skiing is an **open** skill sport where we encounter a potentially infinite number of situations as we venture down the mountain. It is impossible to establish and to train ourselves in the countless number of movements needed to handle any potential situation that might occur. The **openness** of skiing demands that we **ALLOW** our bodies to move in a manner that maintains our balance while letting us execute the intended tactic. Accordingly, understanding the difference between **open** and **closed** skills and the fact that skiing is an **open** skill sport is vital to improving your skiing.

As an example, a 'traditional' **closed** skill approach for someone who is sitting-back while skiing is the often heard advice, "Keep your hands forward." The intention of this forward-hand-positioning directive evolved from observing a typical symptom of sitting-back – the retreating of the skier's hands. However, just having skiers try to move their hands forward only addresses a **symptom**, not the **cause**, of their sitting-back, and generally, doesn't improve their balance. In fact, in many cases, their lack of balancing skills results in their butt moving further back, making the problem worse.

In the case of someone **sitting-back**, the **open** skill approach we use focuses on improving fore-aft balancing skills which is the root of the problem (from the **Prescription Model**). This approach involves performing tasks that allow the person to **feel** what it's like to actually move forward. This addresses the needed skill development directly (using the **Learning Model**). An example of this type of task is trying to keep pressure on the tips of the skis throughout the entire turn (from the **Mechanics Model**). While performing this task, all the skiers' body parts, including their hands, are allowed to move where they need to move to maintain balance. The body shouldn't be **consciously** forced into some pre-programmed position that may or may not be appropriate for the moment at hand. It just so happens that the hands of a person in-balance are generally forward. Understand that, in this **open** skill approach, habitual sitting-back is corrected as a result of performing a task that focuses on improving fore-aft balancing skills, not as a result of trying to perform a pre-programmed movement or drill. **The task becomes the teacher!**

With all its complex elements, learning to ski better is actually pretty simple if you approach it with the understanding that skiing is an **open** skill sport. Learn to let your body move as it needs to move, rather than trying to get it into that picture-perfect pose. Begin by developing the core of good skiing by focusing on improving your balancing skills and using tactics appropriate for your level of skiing. Leave the details for later. The Learning Triad gives you a plan of action and the tools for exactly that approach.

8

Your Equipment Counts

So, you want to get some new or maybe your first set of equipment. Looking at what's out there, the first thing you'll discover is that there are a million choices. Modern technology and materials have made it possible for manufacturers to design and build very specialized ski equipment. To help us make sense of all the choices, they have created different categories that describe where their products fit in the wide performance spectrum. Some examples of these categories include: pure race, all-mountain, on and off-piste, just for women, freeride, twin tips, sport performance, and kids. So, where do we start?

If you are already a good skier, you probably know what category best describes how you ski. In that case, just stick with what has been working for you. If you are a typical recreational skier, or you are not sure what to do, here are some rules of thumb you can follow.

For Skis:

- **ALL-MOUNTAIN skis are the most versatile.** Check out this category first. The new all-mountain skis are just wonderful instruments for gliding over and through the snow. They can carve, skid, and do most anything else you might ask; and they can do it very, very well.

- **Shorter is better than longer.** Unless you ski a lot, like to ski fast, or race, shorter skis are just easier to handle, especially in tough conditions. Even in a shorter length, it's hard to out-ski a good all-mountain ski. For the advanced recreational skier, a ski that reaches somewhere between your nose and forehead is about right.

- **Softer is better than stiffer.** Soft skis give a smoother ride and are a real life-saver in the bumps. And, contrary to common belief, we find that at the speeds most skiers ski, softer skis can actually hold better on hard snow.

- **Wider is better than narrower.** (but not **too** wide for Eastern skiers). An old rule of thumb was that a wide ski was good for powder and a narrow ski was best on hard snow. The modern all-mountain ski has broken that paradigm. As avid skiers, we make a point to ski on a lot of different skis and have been amazed just how well some of the new wider skis hold on 'ice'. So, now we can have the best of both worlds – a ski that floats through the soft snow and crud **and** also holds when you get onto the hard pack. Isn't life wonderful! For all-around skiing, we have found that skis with a waist (that part directly under your foot) in the range of about 76 to 84 mm seem to work great.

- **A medium radius ski generally works best.** If you look at the 'specs' printed on a ski, you will see that every ski has a design radius. Short design radius skis (12 - 13 meters) like to make short, quick turns but aren't at their best when making long, smooth turns. A long radius ski (19 - 22 meters) is just the opposite. These skis like to make long radius turns better than they like to make short radius turns. For most people, skis with a radius of about 14 to 16 meters seem to work best for all-around skiing.

- **Try before you buy.** If you can, it's always better to try before you buy. Most mountains have several 'demo' days per season or may even have a 'demo' center. On the 'demo' days, manufacturers make their skis, and sometimes their boots, available to the public for a few test runs on the snow. And it's all free! These 'demo' days are worth their weight in gold.

For Bindings:

For the most part, modern skis and bindings are sold together as a system. The bindings are typically mounted on rails that are built into the ski. This has really made buying a binding very simple. However, there are some skis that still use the classic screwed-in binding. Either type works fine. Some specifics you need to consider when selecting your binding are:

- **Know your DIN (release) setting.** Your height, weight, age, and skier style determine your DIN or release setting. So, be sure that you're telling the truth when you fill out the form the ski mechanic gives you. Don't worry, baby-boomers, ski mechanics are under a strict code of ethics that forbids them from telling anyone's age. Once you know your setting, choose a binding that puts your DIN number approximately in the middle of the binding's setting range. For example, if you ski with a DIN setting of 5, it is best to pick a binding with a maximum setting of no more than 10 or 12. Don't be tempted to buy that race binding 'on sale' that goes up to a DIN of 17. When you use a binding that is set at the extremes of its adjustment range, you can run the risk of erratic release.

- **Shock absorption.** Shock absorption is the binding's ability to absorb a momentary impact force that is above your DIN setting. While these impact forces don't last long enough to cause an injury, the binding needs to keep your boot attached to the ski. The more shock absorption a binding has, the less chance there is of the binding releasing unnecessarily. Releasing unnecessarily is commonly known as a 'pre-release.' Some lower price bindings have less shock absorption capability than the more expensive models. Buy the most you can afford.

For Boots:

Deciding which boot is right for you is, without a doubt, the most important and, at the same time, the most difficult job of all. Your boot is the connection between your body and the ski. If there's a bad connection, your skis just don't get the message your body is trying to send to them. Besides providing a good connection, a boot needs to be comfortable. Some rules of thumb for boots are:

- **Comfort reigns supreme.** There is nothing worse than poor fitting boots that hurt. If your feet hurt, the only thing you will be able to think about is how fast you can get back in to the lodge and get those boots off. Not a good start to that perfect day on the slopes! Our best advice is to find a good boot fitter close to your home mountain and to be prepared to spend a fair amount of time selecting your boots and getting them properly fit. Keep in mind, there are 'boot fitters' and then there are 'boot fitters.' We recommend finding a **qualified** boot fitter typically found in a boot specialty shop. Qualified boot fitters will closely examine the shape of your feet and discuss your performance needs. With this information, they can narrow down the brands and models that best fit your feet while still meeting your performance expectations. Be warned that boots will feel different in the shop than they will on the snow. Boots that felt like gloves in the shop can turn into vice grips on the snow as the boots get colder and stiffen up. It's best to have your boot fitter near-by because a minor adjustment may be all that's needed.

- **Smaller is better than bigger.** Believe it or not, most people have boots that are too big. Oversize boots sure feel good in the shop; however, boots that are too big severely limit your ability to control your skis. As a rule, you should choose the smallest shell that **comfortably** fits your foot. Boots have two major components: the hard plastic outer shell and the soft inner bladder. The shells are generally made in full-size increments while the bladders are made in half-size increments. A good boot fitter will always remove the bladder from the boot in order to check the fit of your foot in the shell. Then, with your foot in the shell and your toes touching at the front, he will measure the distance between your heel and the back of the boot. A distance of no more than 3/4 inch is considered a good recreational fit.

- **Custom footbeds rule.** Knowledgeable boot fitters will almost always suggest that you get custom footbeds (orthotics) molded specifically to your feet. Custom footbeds have two major purposes: first and foremost, they serve as the foundation for proper support and alignment of your skeleton; and second, they help secure your feet inside your boots improving the connection between your body and your skis. A proper set of custom footbeds is well worth the investment.

- **Align it up.** Part of the boot fitting experience and a good boot fitter's skill is getting your boots properly aligned with your legs. This involves adjusting and possibly shimming and/or grinding your boots both for canting (shaft alignment) and balancing (ramp angle adjustment). Having your boots properly aligned greatly enhances your ability to find and maintain balance on your skis. **GETTING PROPERLY ALIGNED IS AN ABSOLUTE MUST IF YOU WANT TO SKI CONSISTENTLY AT AN ADVANCED LEVEL**.

- **Softer is better than stiffer.** Just as with the softer skis, a softer boot works better for most recreational skiers. Effective skiing requires that your ankles be free to flex. An overly stiff boot limits that flex and inhibits your ability to find and maintain your balance. This is one of the major reasons people sit back when they ski. When selecting your boots, keep in mind that boots will stiffen up as they get colder. Boots that may seem soft in the shop can quickly get too stiff out on the hill. When out in the cold, you should be able to flex your ankles enough so that the front of your knees move forward, at least to the front of the binding toe piece. A good boot fitter should be able to modify boots that are too stiff to make them ski softer.

For Poles:

When choosing poles, you should look for a pole that is light in weight, easy to swing, and correct in length.

- **Lighter is better.** Heavy poles can slow down your arm movements. This, in turn, affects your ability to stay in-balance. Plus, they're exhausting to use!

- **A tisket a tasket, what size basket?** Poles come with a variety of basket sizes. As a general rule, we use small baskets for packed, groomed trails to help reduce swing weight. We use larger diameter baskets for softer, deeper snow to help prevent the pole from sinking too deeply into the snow. A medium size basket works OK for most recreational skiers.

- **The long and short of it.** In the shop, you can easily check for correct pole length by placing the pole's grip on the floor and grasping the pole shaft just under the basket. If your forearm is close to being parallel with the floor, the pole is the right length.

- **Strap it up.** Unless you are skiing in the woods where catching your pole basket can wrench your arm, it's best to use the pole straps. The straps provide added support and can help prevent you from losing a pole, particularly in deep snow. Poles generally come with either a standard nylon strap that loops around your glove or a device that clips your pole to your glove. Either works fine. It's just a matter of personal choice.

For Helmets:

What's the scoop with helmets? Today's helmets are designed to protect your head from direct impacts of less than about 15 MPH.

"But, I ski much faster than that," you say, "so why bother?" It's simple. While a helmet may not offer all that much protection in a direct, high-speed collision, it works great for protecting against glancing blows. In these situations, it can be a lifesaver. As they say, an ounce of prevention is worth a pound of cure.

- **Snug it up.** Since both helmets and heads come in all shapes and sizes, start the fitting process by finding your general size. That's easy. Helmet sizes are given in centimeters that correspond to the circumference of your head as measured across your forehead. Once you have your helmet size, try it on to make sure the helmet's shape suits the shape of your head. A correctly fitting helmet should be snug, but not uncomfortably tight.

- **Don't forget your goggles.** Be sure that your goggles fit with your helmet. Helmets can change the way your goggles rest on your face. Have your goggles with you when you buy your new helmet to make sure it all fits together.

- **Up to the Standard.** Before you buy, check to see that the helmet meets the current industry safety standards set by the ASTM (American Society for Testing and Materials) and CEN (Central European Norm). Most brand name manufacturers test their products in accordance with these standards, but it doesn't hurt to look for the seal.

A word of caution! Be careful about buying equipment just because you saw a good skier using it. What's good for that skier might not be the best choice for you. Also, remember, while most of us look for bargains, buying on price alone can leave you very disappointed. When properly maintained, quality equipment will not only perform well for you, but will also last for years.

9

Let Your Skis Do The Work - You Paid Enough For Them! -

Skiing is like playing the piano. Some people can only play chopsticks, some can play Beethoven, and the rest fall somewhere in-between. The 'best' piano players look to play on the 'best' pianos. They know how to use the piano as the instrument it was designed to be, milking every sweet note from its ivory keys. People who can only play chopsticks don't really care what kind of piano they're using. And, unless they want to get better, it really doesn't matter. Clearly, for the better piano players, their equipment counts. People who want to improve their piano playing soon learn that the better the piano, the better the outcome. And so it is with skiing. Your ski equipment affects the kind of song you will be able to play on your skis. If all you want to do is swish the tails of your skis from side to side, braking your speed with every swish (the same as playing chopsticks on your skis), it really doesn't matter what you ski on. For this kind of skiing, even the old straight skis would work OK. However, if you want to play something with a bit more pizzazz, your equipment does matter. In **Chapter 8, Your Equipment Counts,** we go over how to tackle the task of choosing ski equipment that's best suited for you.

Modern skis are designed to turn, and the ski manufacturers have gone overboard trying to make the most of modern materials and technology to that end. The result is that the best of the new skis can respond to your every whim. Here's where you need to understand that the ski only does what you tell it to do. The task then becomes learning how to talk to your skis so they do what you want them to do, when you want them to do it. Just as when you converse with another person, so it is as you ski, you and your skis need to speak the same language. If you remember in **Chapter 2, It's All About Balance!,** the language of skiing is **balance**. Learn to balance and you've learned the language. Once you can talk to your skis, you just need to tell them what you want them to do. Then, enjoy the ride and let the skis do the work.

Most skiers think of skiing as making one turn, then another, then another, and so on. This approach often leads to a series of disjointed, mechanical, and pre-programmed movements. Typically, the result of this thinking is a quick twisting of the skis across the fall line ending with a skidded braking move. Twist the ski, then put on the brakes! In the ski teaching business, we call this a 'Z' turn. A better approach is to simply follow a path and just **GO PLACES**. A long turn is just going to places that are far apart. A short turn is going to places that are close together. This approach makes life so much simpler. All you need to do is to choose a path down the hill, then follow that path going from place to place, changing direction whenever and wherever you need or want.

To get an idea of how this might work, imagine you are on your bike on the top of a trail. The trail is paved and your bike doesn't have any brakes. How would you get down? Simple. You would start down the hill, going from place to place, along a path that would control your speed. The path you choose would most likely start down the hill, with a change in direction across the hill, and possibly slightly back up the hill until your speed is under control. This path would continue all the way to the bottom. You would be changing direction depending upon the steepness of the hill, the speed you want to travel, and any obstacles that might be in your way. The result would be a series of smooth, seamless, controlled changes of direction. In skiing, we call this making **round** turns. The fun part here is that you would not be thinking about what movements you're making. You would just be balancing on your bike, going from place to place. You would be telling your bike what to do and it would be listening. You and your bike are speaking the same language. Now, just do that on your skis!

As you learn to ski along a path (making round turns), it's very important that you learn to **feel** when your direction changes – that moment of transition between going in one and then the other direction. At that moment, you just get the feeling that you're 'going' in the other direction without actually having 'turned' your skis. If you're not skiing along a path, you will surely have to move your skis sideways before you feel any direction change. Following a 'bicycle' type path down the hill results in a style that is totally opposite from the 'Z' turn style of skiing we talked about earlier.

One common trait of good skiers is that they all seem to love the fall line – that moment in the turn where their skis are pointing straight down the hill. The lure of the fall line, I believe, comes from the unique confluence of gravity, speed, and sensation that only occurs when your skis are following that part of the path. Modern ski design has only enhanced the quality of that experience.

One of the best parts about skiing a **path** is that changing your skis' direction becomes almost effortless. You are letting the skis do the work. Skiing this way gives you the feeling and the freedom to play any song you want!

10

Tasks Every 'Good' Skier Can Do

If you remember in **Chapter 5, Supercharge Your Learning,** we spoke about tasks and how we can use them to supercharge our learning. Those tasks were simply activity in the quest of a specific outcome. Get in the habit of watching really good skiers. You will notice that there are certain tasks that they all can do. These tasks require good fore-aft, lateral, and vertical balancing skills, as well as an effective tactical approach. It makes sense, then, to practice these tasks.

The best of these tasks are those we call **self-assessing tasks**. A self-assessing task is one that, when you try it, you don't need anyone to tell you whether or not you did it correctly. A good example is a shot taken in basketball. No one has to tell you whether or not the ball goes in the basket: you just have to look and see for yourself. What could be simpler? While there are a number of tasks we might try while skiing, we have found four that we use all the time for training because they are especially effective. Here they are:

- **The downhill ski traverse** – the ability to leave a clean, narrow track in the snow with the downhill ski while traversing across the hill. This is a fundamental skill of every good skier. The best part is all you have to do is look back at your track to see if you did it. It is amazing how many skiers cannot perform this seemingly simple task. If you need to practice something, practice this first! This task is great for developing fore-aft and lateral balance, as well as edging and pressure control skills.

- **Ski with 100% of your weight on the outside ski of the turn** – This task expands the skills of the downhill ski traverse into a turn. Until you learn to balance on the outside ski, you will forever be stuck in skiers' limbo. Practice this task to the point that you can lift the inside ski completely off the snow. When done correctly there should not be any change in your lateral balance as your inside ski is lifted. A note of caution – most people tend to fall toward the inside of the turn when they lift up the inside ski. Pay special attention to this, as falling or tipping to the inside is a sure sign of being out of lateral balance.

- **Keep the tips of your skis engaged in the snow throughout the entire turn** – Sitting-back, or what we call skiing in the 'backseat' is probably the most common problem skiers have. Learning to keep the tips engaged in the snow will cure any 'backseat' problems. It is impossible to keep the tips of the skis engaged in the snow if you are sitting-back. Good skiers almost always start a turn with tip engagement and then, in the turn, decide where along the ski they want the pressure to be – sometimes they keep it toward the tip, sometimes they move it to the middle, or sometimes they may even move it toward the tail of the ski. It all depends on the specific situation. It's only when you learn to get and stay forward do you have the option to vary the pressure anywhere along the ski. The feeling you get when you actually engage the tips of the skis in the snow is one that will both surprise and please you. The ski literally turns by itself. It's designed to do just that!

- **Make turns on the same ski in both directions** – This is one of the greatest tasks for learning what it feels like to move forward into the turn. In this task, keep 99% of your weight on the same ski all the time, whether you are turning to the right or to the left. The **other** ski should just be touching the snow for balance. If you are standing on the left ski, the turn to the right is typically easy. However, while standing on the left ski trying to make the turn to the left, the ski just doesn't turn if you don't move forward. Instant feedback! When first attempting this task, you will be amazed how far forward you feel you have to move in order to make the ski go around the corner. But, when you get that feeling, watch out. Breakthrough time is here! This task sets up effective use of the inside ski – a hallmark of the advanced skier. On a personal note, this task has to be the eye opener of the year for me (Joan). Frankly, I was getting tired of hearing, "Move forward, move into the turn, and/or dive down the hill." I also heard, "Throw yourself down the hill!" Let's get real here! How far? How much? Of course, I tried to do all of these things, at least to the degree that my frightened little body would let me. But, when I did this one-footed turn task, I was dumbfounded with what happened. When I tried to turn to the right standing on my right foot or to the left standing on my left foot, it just didn't happen until I REALLY moved forward into the new turn. I finally felt what moving into the turn was really like! The self-assessing part of this task is simple – the ski either turns or it doesn't. Personally, if there is one task that I really like, it is this one.

As an aside, most of the tasks we use in our training sessions are skiing-type tasks that transfer directly into a person's 'regular' skiing. Generally, we have found this to be more productive than the use of exercises that attempt to isolate one skill with a practiced movement pattern. Considering the **openness** of skiing, see **Chapter 1, Throw Away Your Checklist**, exercises seem to be more of a test of one's ability rather than an open skill development tool. Remember – **LET THE TASK BE THE TEACHER!**

11

Forward, Forward, Forward!

In this book we keep harping on the need to continually 'move forward' as you ski. As trainers and instructors, we find that getting someone to learn how to **move forward** is one of the hardest things to do. So, how might you approach learning this elusive skill? It is interesting to note that moving forward requires a blend of fore-aft and lateral balancing skills as well as the ability to move independently from ski to ski.

First, understand there is a big difference between **leaning** forward and **moving** forward. However, that being said, our work often begins with learning to ski while leaning forward; and then we work with those sensations to further develop the feeling of actually moving forward.

We have had good success using the following series of tasks:

- Start by skiing on a green trail imagining that someone has cut off the tails of your skis. Your **home** fore-aft stance should be at, or forward of, the ball of your foot. As you make your turns, you should feel the tips of your skis constantly pressing into the snow. You might also notice that it becomes easier to keep your speed under control and to change direction. These sensations become the seed of **Move to Engage the Tips** outlined in **The Simplified Mechanics of Skiing** in **Chapter 3**.

    After practicing this for a while, you need to make sure your lateral balancing skills are up to par. Practicing skiing with 100% of your weight on the outside ski of the turn (the second task listed in **Chapter 10**) would be good here.

- When you can reasonably balance on your outside ski, the next task to practice is what we call **Stuff the Tip**. This task involves taking the tip of the uphill (new turning) ski and pushing it forward on its inside edge into the fall line while continuing to balance on the downhill ski. Allow your weight to transfer to the new turning ski as the tip engages the snow. The new turn should start automatically. Keep the turn going by continuously driving the tips of both skis forward along the path of the turn. Regain your stance by finding **home** on the outside ski and begin again.

What's great about this series of tasks is how the feeling of **leaning** forward evolves into **moving** forward. This feeling happens as you master **stuffing the tip** of the new turning ski into the fall line. You will find that you can't **stuff the tip** if you aren't moving forward.

Don't fret if, when you first try this progression, your outside ski stems a bit. The important thing here is to get the feeling of starting the turn by moving forward and engaging the tip of the new outside ski in the snow. Once that feeling is established, spend your time practicing skiing on one foot (the fourth task in **Chapter 10, Tasks Every 'Good" Skier Can Do**). You will soon be able to engage the tips of both skis simultaneously at the start of your turns.

So learn to **Stuff the Tip** and feel what happens!

12

Tactics are the Pieces – Balance is the Glue

As a skier, even if you have all the skiing skills in the world, the choice of inappropriate tactics will often lead to disaster. According to Merriam Webster, 'tactics' is defined as "The art or skill of employing available means to accomplish an end." What a great definition for us skiers! However, reading this definition does make one realize that there is an infinite number of potential tactics that can be used. As we mentioned in **Chapter 2, It's All About Balance!,** being able to maintain a state of dynamic balance allows us to do what we want, when we want, where we want. This cannot be overstated as, without good balancing skills, tactics become more of an accident rather than a choice. With that understanding, it's clear that there is a definitive link between the skill of balancing and the execution of a tactic. Think about tactics as being the pieces of your run and your balancing skills as the glue that holds them together.

The **path** we choose is the most fundamental tactical choice we make as we ski down the hill. Almost all other tactics emanate from that choice. You can see how skiing a particular path down a hill covered with two feet of new snow would require a much different approach than when skiing the same path when it's icy. With your path selected, the focus of your tactical choices becomes dependant upon the conditions of the hill, the weather, your equipment, skier traffic, etc. However, remembering that skiing is an **open skill**, the actual tactical choice we make at any particular moment needs to be based on the situation at hand. Understand that we need to approach tactics more holistically, rather than trying to focus on making specific movements.

As a case in point – I was skiing with our snow sports school director in some particularly heavy, bumped-up crud. As I was getting knocked about, I watched him snake effortlessly through the bumps and wondered how he did that. Riding back up the lift, I asked him, "What are you trying to do in this stuff?" He thought for a moment and said, "I just try to keep my skis turning." He didn't say he tried to keep his hands forward, bend his knees more, or any of those typical **closed skill** analysis comments. His approach was more holistic, "I just keep turning my skis." When we got to the top, we skied the same trail again; only this time, I didn't worry about anything except constantly turning my skis. The difference in my skiing was amazing. As I danced through the crud, it 'seemed' as though they had just groomed the trail. This simple, tactical change made a world of difference in the way I could respond to the conditions at hand. After we went in, I sat down and thought about what had happened. Although I didn't think about it when I was skiing, the technical changes in my skiing resulting from that simple, tactical change proved to be significant. In order to keep my skis turning in that deep, heavy snow,

I had to ski a flatter ski with less edging than before. This allowed my skis to slice more smoothly through the snow. Also, as my skis turned under me, they allowed my body to keep moving down the hill without my getting knocked into the backseat. The best part was that all this **good stuff** just **happened**.

There is one thing that is undeniable – you need to **ski** to get better at skiing. Nothing beats experience; and surely, my director's vast experience has taught him how to approach a wide variety of situations. However, if you take home anything from this story, let it be that my director did not tell me how to keep my skis turning or what movements I needed to make. He simply gave me a tactical outcome and let **me** take it from there. After my work with Kolb's model, I instinctively cycled myself through the four stages of his model; and it took me only a few turns to figure it out. The choice of tactics changed my whole skiing experience.

So, what does the inexperienced skier do – the skier who does not have the vast experience of my director? These skiers need to simply focus on maintaining balance and to be willing to try many different approaches until they find a tactic that works, whether it is the path they follow, the speed they choose, or the type of turn they decide to make. These skiers will discover that, at times, they will do things they have never done before. Of course, it can also help if they ski with an experienced skier who can help narrow down the possibilities.

While it would be impossible to list all the tactical choices that might be available as we ski, we have ventured to list some choices you might consider. We have done this so you might better understand how to approach choosing a particular tactic for a particular situation. Please understand that what we have listed is not intended to be the only way to approach a situation. They are offered only as starting points for your own exploration.

Steep slopes: For less experienced skiers, a steep slope is any slope where the thought of changing direction is intimidating, sometimes to the point where they can't move. Here is when a specific tactical approach can make all the difference in the world. Case in point – We were skiing down an intermediate slope when we came upon a young woman sitting on the snow in the middle of the trail, crying. Her boyfriend was standing about fifty yards down the trail yelling to her, "Just get up and ski down!" (Not a good moment in their relationship.) As we skied over to her, I asked, "Can I help you?" She said, "It's way too steep: I can't ski down here." Seeing my snow sports school jacket, she seemed relieved to see me. As we sat together on the snow talking, I convinced her to stand up. Once we were standing, I told her that it was not that the trail was steep, it was just that she didn't understand it. I then explained that, "A steep hill is nothing more than a flat hill that's tilted." This bizarre comment got her attention! I'm sure she was wondering what she had gotten herself into. My goal, in fact, was to take her mind off the steepness of the trail; and it worked. I continued to explain that because it started out as a flat hill, it still had lots of 'flat spots' on it. All we had to do was find the 'flat spots' and ski them (a tactic). I showed her a 'flat spot' – a path that would take her directly across the hill. After getting her to balance towards the front of her downhill ski, I asked her to ski the 'flat spot' all the way across the hill (another tactic). Focusing on the 'flat spot' changed her perception of the hill. She did it without a hitch. When we got to the side of the trail and stopped, she realized that she needed to go the other way. She trusted me now; so when I asked her to point her uphill ski straight down the hill, stand on it, and find the 'flat spot' in the other direction, she took a long, hard look at me, took a deep breath, and did exactly what I asked her to do (still another tactic). As she skied from 'flat spot' to 'flat spot,' she went right past her boyfriend and skied all the way down to the lift. When we got to the bottom, she thanked me and got right back on the lift to do it again. What I like about this story is that it only took a change in tactics to completely change this young woman's skiing. Tactics saved the day! (I'm not too sure about her relationship with her boyfriend!)

Ice: If you ski anywhere in the East, ice is just another one of those conditions you need to learn to live with. One thing for sure, if you don't have sharp skis, get ready to **pivot and slip**. That's about the only tactic that works. However, when sharp, most modern skis will hold well enough to ski a reasonable path in icy snow. Getting them to hold, though, requires that you get your skis on a high edge, away from your body. This is when decent lateral balancing skills are essential. Depending upon what **you** want to happen, whether you ski with pressure on one ski or on both skis, is a matter of choice. Personally, when I really want my skis to hold, I find putting most of my weight on my outside ski works best (a tactic). Skiing with weight on both skis, however, makes it easier for me to ski a shaped, somewhat skidded turn (another tactic).

One bit of advice that we often hear is to let go of some of the pressure on your skis to make them hold better on ice. While this may give you the sensation that your skis are holding better, actually, this sensation is the result of a reduction of the turning force applied to your skis. While your skis may track better, the size of your turn necessarily gets larger. This larger turn, however, may not adequately control your speed. If speed control is an issue, this tactic is not a good choice. On slopes where speed is not an issue, this tactic may be acceptable.

When conditions really get slippery, my favorite tactic is simply – "If they don't hold, let'em slip."

Bumps: So you want to learn to ski the bumps? With that in mind, you might think the first thing you need to do is jump right into them and tough it out. In actuality, the first thing you need to do is to build a strong tactical foundation on **groomed** slopes. It's on the groomed slopes where you can hone your tactical skills so they can be applied in the bumps when and where they're needed. Building that tactical foundation, of course, assumes your balancing skills are reasonably well-developed. The ability to **find home** as we describe in **Chapter 2, It's All About Balance!,** becomes an essential first skill. If you have trouble maintaining your balance, skiing the bumps will be a real challenge, to say the least, and probably not a lot of fun.

If you have spent any time trying to ski the bumps, you probably know what it feels like to get knocked into the backseat – that moment when you are hanging on for dear life with your skis shooting out in front of you, without any chance of changing direction. We all have experienced it and *it ain't no fun!* So, learning to move forward toward the front of your skis, as we describe throughout this book, becomes an essential tactical skill in the bumps. Practice this one a lot!

Although modern skis are built to carve, forget carving in the bumps. In the bumps, slipping is the way to go. Tactically, for the bumps, you need to develop a bulletproof forward sideslip. A forward sideslip allows you to control your speed and also gives you the ability to better adjust your line (path) as you try to navigate through those scary mounds of snow.

The ability to pivot your skis is another tactical skill you need to have to ski the bumps. Many times, particularly when the bumps are close together and you need to change direction quickly, being able to pivot your skis can really help you make those quick direction changes.

With this foundation, it's time to venture into the bumps. Now, comes the application – making those actual tactical choices as you ski. As we mentioned before, the path you choose is the most fundamental tactical choice you will make. This is particularly true in the bumps. While there are numerous paths that you might take in the bumps, they generally fall into two categories – the zipper line (skiing in the troughs between the bumps) and the high line (skiing up and over the bumps). The zipper line is a fast line, in the fall line, where the size and shape of each turn is dictated by the shape of the bumps. This line is best left to the bump aficionados. For the rest of us, a high line, up, over, and around the bumps is a more conservative tactical choice that provides many more options. A little extra insight here, bumps on the side of a trail are usually not as ominous as those in the middle of the trail.

With a path selected, we have found that following a basic tactical sequence in the bumps helps to set you up for success. That sequence is – find home, move forward, then turn your skis. As we stated earlier, "If you're not in-balance, nothing else matters." **Finding home** first puts you in-balance and ready for whatever comes next.

Sitting back in the bumps can be deadly. Not only will you lose any sense of speed control; but also, when you try to change direction, the tails of your skis will very often get caught on a bump. **Moving forward** prevents all that from happening. It allows you to turn your skis when and where you want. (Hint: it helps if you ski from a slightly taller stance). So the last element of the sequence is **turn your skis**. At this point, it becomes your choice – pivot 'em, skid 'em, or just turn 'em.

Powder and Crud: Just like learning to ski the bumps, learning to ski powder and crud starts with a strong tactical foundation. This includes developing the ability to adapt your fore-aft and lateral balance to the snow conditions and to shape a round turn. 'Z' turns just don't work very well in powder and crud. Tactically, it's best to ski a narrower stance with equal weight on each ski. Just try to ski with both skis as a single unit and keep actively turning your skis. When you stop turning your skis, they get a mind of their own and they start wandering off in all directions! As an aside, wider skis are a big help in these conditions.

Because the depth of the snow helps to control your speed in powder, a more direct path down the fall line works best. On open slopes, skiing a rhythm also helps. In the crud, skiing through the clumps helps control your speed. You just have to be ready for the stop-and-go feeling that makes crud challenging. Try thinking about punching a hole in a clump of snow with the tips of your skis and ski your boots through the hole. It's fun to do and it helps shape your turn.

If you find yourself in one of those situations where the snow might be too deep and the slope a little too steep, try the good ole, reliable wedge turn with a tweak – rise up into a wedge as you steer your skis into the fall line. Then, sink down to complete your turn with your skis parallel. The active up and down allows your skis to **work** in the snow and the steering augments your direction change.

As an aside, Joanie always says she has an advantage in the powder because, "The shorter you are, the deeper the powder!"

"The shorter you are –
the deeper the powder"

Wrap Up

When all is said and done, skiing better does take some time and effort; however, at its core, skiing is basically simple. Balance on your skis, choose your path, and let your movements evolve. Understand that skiing is an **open skill** sport where every moment offers a new and different challenge. Knowing this allows you to ski in the moment, in the **NOW.** Approaching skiing as an open skill frees you to dance down the hill, playing with the snow and terrain in a spontaneous choreography of movement controlled only by your imagination and the willingness of the mountain to cooperate.

For years, our goal has been trying to answer the question, "Why does learning to ski better take so long?" Fortunately, with the help of Professor Kolb and his Experiential Learning Model, we have discovered how to supercharge the learning process. And, by combining Kolb's learning model with a simple mechanics model and an easy-to-use prescriptive tool, learning really explodes.   Our experience with this combination can only be described as amazing.

While we have had great success with our approach, we continue to evolve the process. Our work now focuses on optimizing task progressions and working on more effective ways to get skiers into the experiential learning cycle. Kolb's first stage (feeler) is undoubtedly a crucial starting place. We are always searching for better ways to get learners to enter this stage even though their dominant learning style is not that of a feeler. Because learners typically favor a dominant learning style, more often than not, they are hesitant to learn how to learn in the other styles. Take the leap and 'learn to learn' in all four styles.

We are constantly faced with the seduction of the "What am I doing wrong?" approach. It is here where the learner wants to be given the secret handshake. In truth, there is no secret handshake. Surely, while there are basic fundamentals to good skiing, everybody needs to find what works for them. Learning to combine function and style is the hallmark of a great skier. Hopefully, our work will help you make the jump to great skiing!

About David A. Kolb

David A. Kolb is an American educational theorist whose research and publications focus on experiential learning and learning styles. He is the founder and chairman of Experience Based Learning Systems, Inc. (EBLS) and a Professor of Organizational Behavior in the Weatherhead School of Management, Case Western Reserve University, Cleveland, Ohio.

Professor Kolb earned his BA from Knox College in 1961 and his MA and PH.D. from Harvard University in 1964 and 1967, respectively, in social psychology. In the early 1970's, Professor Kolb developed his Experiential Learning Theory and the Learning Cycle. He named the theory to emphasize its links to ideas from John Dewey, Jean Piaget, Kurt Lewin, and other writers from the experiential learning paradigm. His model was developed predominately for use with adult learners but has found widespread teaching implications in higher education. More information about his work can be found at www.learningfromexperience.com.